# ODE TO
# childhood

## POETRY TO CELEBRATE THE CHILD

Edited by Lucy Gray

**BATSFORD**

First published in the United Kingdom in 2014 by
Batsford
10 Southcombe Street
London W14 0RA

An imprint of Anova Books Ltd

This book is based on *The Poetry of Childhood* (Batsford, 1981)

ISBN: 9781849941334

A CIP catalogue record for this book is available from the
British Library.

20 19 18 17 16 15 14
10 9 8 7 6 5 4 3 2 1

Repro by Mission Productions, Hong Kong
Printed by 1010 Printing International Ltd, China

This book can be ordered direct from the publisher at the website:
www.anovabooks.com, or try your local bookshop.

# Contents

PRIVATE

FOR QUOTATIONS
APPLY
PRIVATE HIRE DEPARTMENT
31, BROADWAY,
WESTMINSTER

# Infant Joy

'I have no name;
I am but two days old.'
What shall I call thee?
'I happy am,
Joy is my name.'
Sweet joy befall thee!

Pretty joy!
Sweet joy, but two days old.
Sweet Joy I call thee:
Thou dost smile,
I sing the while;
Sweet joy befall thee!

**William Blake**
(1757–1827)

# The Baby's Dance

Dance, little baby, dance up high,
Never mind baby, mother is by;
Crow and caper, caper and crow,
There little baby, there you go:
Up to the ceiling, down to the ground,
Backwards and forwards, round and round.
Then dance, little baby, and mother shall sing,
With the merry gay coral, ding, ding, a-ding, ding.

Ann Taylor
(1782–1866)

# Things like Ourselves

from: The Mad Lover

Things like ourselves, as sensual, vain, invented
Bubbles, and breaths of air, got with an itching,
As blisters are and bred; as much corruption
Flows from their lives: sorrow conceives and shapes 'em;
And oftentimes the death of those we love most.
The breeders bring 'em to the World to curse 'em,
Crying they creep amongst us like young Cats.
Cares and continual crosses keeping with 'em.
They make Time old to tend them, and experience
An ass: they alter so; they grow, and goodly,
Ere we can turn our thoughts, like drops of water
They fall into the main, and are known no more;
This is the love of this World; I must tell thee
For thou art understanding.

Francis Beaumont
(1584–1616)
and
John Fletcher
(1579–1625)

My daughter cries, and I
Lift her from where she lies,
Carry her here and there,
Talk nonsense endlessly.
And still she cries and cries
In rage, mindlessly.

A trivial anguish, found
In every baby-book.
But, at a fortnight old,
A pink and frantic mound
Of appetites, each look
Scans unfamiliar ground.

A name without a face
Becomes a creature, takes
A creature's energies.
Raging in my embrace.
She takes the world and shakes
Each firm appointed place.

No language blocks her way,
Oblique, loaded with tact.
Hunger and pain are real,
And in her blindness they
Are all she sees: the fact
Is what you cannot say.

Our difference is that
We gauge what each cry says,
Supply what need demands.
Or try to. All falls flat
If cure is wrong or guess
Leaves her still obdurate.

So through uncertainties
I carry her here and there,
And feel her human heart,
Her human miseries,
And in her language share
Her blind and trivial cries.

Anthony Thwaite
(1930– )

# Characteristics of a Child Three Years Old

Loving she is, and tractable, though wild;
And Innocence hath privilege in her
To dignify arch looks and laughing eyes;
And feats of cunning; and the pretty round
Of trespasses, affected to provoke
Mock-chastisement and partnership in play.
And, as a faggot sparkles on the hearth,
Not less if unattended and alone
Than when both young and old sit gathered round
And take delight in its activity;
Even so this happy Creature of herself
Is all-sufficient, solitude to her
Is blithe society, who fills the air
With gladness and involuntary songs.
Light are her sallies as the tripping fawn's
Forth-startled from the fern where she lay couched;
Unthought-of, unexpected, as the stir
Of the soft breeze ruilling the meadow-flowers,
Or from before it chasing wantonly
The many-coloured images imprest
Upon the bosom of a placid lake.

William Wordsworth
(1770–1850)

# On a Child Beginning to Talk

Methinks 'tis pretty sport to hear a child
Rocking a word in mouth yet undefiled;
The tender racket rudely plays the sound,
Which, weakly bandied, cannot back rebound.
And the soft air the softer roof doth kiss,
With a sweet dying and a pretty miss,
Which hears no answer yet from the white rank
Of teeth, not risen from their coral bank.
The alphabet is searched for letters soft,
To try a word before it can be wrought;
And, when it slideth forth, it goes as nice
As when a man doth walk upon the ice.

Thomas Bastard
(1566–1618)

# Four Years Old–
# A Nursery Song

One cannot turn a minute,
But mischief—there you're in it,
A-getting at my books, John,
With mighty bustling looks, John;
Or poking at the roses
In midst of which your nose is;
Or climbing on a table,
No matter how unstable,
And turning up your quaint eye
And half-shut teeth with 'Mayn't I?'
Or else you're off at play, John,
Just as you'd be all day, John,
With hat or not, as happens,
And there you dance, and clap hands,
Or on the grass go rolling,
Or plucking flowers, or bowling,
And getting me expenses
With losing balls o'er fences;

But see, the sun shines brightly;
Come, put your hat on rightly,
And we'll among the bushes,
And hear your friends the thrushes.
And see what flow'rs the weather
Has render'd fit to gather;
And, when we home must jog, you
Shall ride my back, you rogue you.
Your hat adorn'd with fir-leaves,
Horse-chestnut, oak, and vine-leaves;
And so, with green o'erhead, John,
Shall whistle home to bed, John.

Leigh Hunt
(1784–1859)

# On Children

How dull our days, how lacking in surprise
Without these small epitomes of sin,
These flowers with their store of life within
And grave, appalling freshness in their eyes.

Frances Cornford
(1886–1960)

# Child and Mother

from: On Receipt of My Mother's picture out of Norfolk

Where once we dwelt our name is heard no more,
Children not thine have trod my nurs'ry floor;
And where the gard'ner Robin, day by day,
Drew me to school along the public way,
Delighted with my bauble coach, and wrapt
In scarlet mantle warm, and velvet capt,
'Tis now become a history little known,

That once we call'd the past'ral house our own.
Short-liv'd possession! but the record fair
That mem'ry keeps of all thy kindness there,
Still outlives many a storm that has effac'd
A thousand other themes less deeply trac'd.
Thy nightly visits to my chamber made,
That thou might'st know me safe and warmly laid;
Thy morning bounties ere I left my home,
The biscuit, or confectionary plum;
The fragrant waters on my cheeks bestow'd
By thy own hand, till fresh they shone and glow'd:
All this, and more endearing still than all,
Thy constant flow of love, that knew no fall,
Ne'er roughen'd by those cataracts and breaks,
That humour interpos'd too often makes;
All this still legible in mem'ry's page,
And still to be so, to my latest age,
Adds joy to duty, makes me glad to pay
Such honours to thee as my numbers may;
Perhaps a frail memorial, but sincere,
Not scorn'd in heav'n, though little notic'd here.

   Could time, his flight revers'd, restore the hours
When, playing with thy vesture's tissued flow'rs
The violet, the pink, and jessamine,
I prick'd them into paper with a pin,
(And thou wast happier than myself the while,
Would'st softly speak, and stroke my head, and smile)
Could those few pleasant hours again appear,
Might one wish bring them, would I wish them here?
I would not trust my heart—the dear delight
Seems so to be desir'd, perhaps I might.

But no:—what here we call our life is such,
So little to be lov'd, and thou so much,
That I should ill requite thee to constrain
Thy unbound spirit into bonds again.

William Cowper
(1731–1800)

# A Child Ill

Oh, little body, do not die.
The soul looks out through wide blue eyes
So questioningly into mine,
That my tormented soul replies:

'Oh, little body, do not die.
You hold the soul that talks to me
Although our conversation be
As wordless as the windy sky.'

So looked my father at the last
Right in my soul, before he died.
Though words we spoke went heedless past
As London traffic-roar outside.

And now the same blue eyes I see
Look through me from a little son,
So questioning, so searchingly
That youthfulness and age are one.

My father looked at me and died
Before my soul made full reply.
Lord, leave this other Light alight
Oh, little body, do not die.

John Betjeman
(1906–1984)

# Frost at Midnight

The Frost performs its secret ministry,
Unhelped by any wind. The owlet's cry
Came loud—and hark, again! loud as before.
The inmates of my cottage, all at rest,
Have left me to that solitude, which suits
Abstruser musings: save that at my side
My cradled infant slumbers peacefully.
'Tis calm indeed! so calm, that it disturbs
And vexes meditation with its strange
And extreme silentness. Sea, hill, and wood,
This populous village! Sea, and hill, and wood,
With all the numberless goings-on of life,
Inaudible as dreams! the thin blue flame
Lies on my low-burnt fire, and quivers not;
Only that film, which fluttered on the grate,

Still flutters there, the sole unquiet thing.
Methinks, its motion in this hush of nature
Gives it dim sympathies with me who live,
Making it a companionable form,
Whose puny flaps and freaks the idling Spirit
By its own moods interprets, every where
Echo or mirror seeking of itself,
And makes a toy of Thought.

         But O! how oft,
How oft, at school, with most believing mind,
Presageful, have I gazed upon the bars,
To watch that fluttering *stranger*! and as oft
With unclosed lids, already had I dreamt

Of my sweet birth-place, and the old church-tower,
Whose bells, the poor man's only music, rang
From morn to evening, all the hot Fair-day,
So sweetly, that they stirred and haunted me
With a wild pleasure, falling on mine ear
Most like articulate sounds of things to come!
So gazed I, till the soothing things, I dreamt,
Lulled me to sleep, and sleep prolonged my dreams!
And so I brooded all the following morn,
Awed by the stern preceptor's face, mine eye
Fixed with mock study on my swimming book:
Save if the door half opened, and I snatched
A hasty glance, and still my heart leaped up,
For still I hoped to see the *stranger's* face,
Townsman, or aunt, or sister more beloved,
My play-mate when we both were clothed alike!

Dear Babe, that sleepest cradled by my side,
Whose gentle breathings, heard in this deep calm,
Fill up the interspersèd vacancies
And momentary pauses of the thought!
My babe so beautiful! it thrills my heart
With tender gladness, thus to look at thee,
And think that thou shalt learn far other lore,
And in far other scenes! For I was reared
In the great city, pent 'mid cloisters dim,
And saw nought lovely but the sky and stars.
But *thou*, my babe! shalt wander like a breeze
By lakes and sandy shores, beneath the crags
Of ancient mountain, and beneath the clouds,
Which image in their bulk both lakes and shores
And mountain crags: so shalt thou see and hear

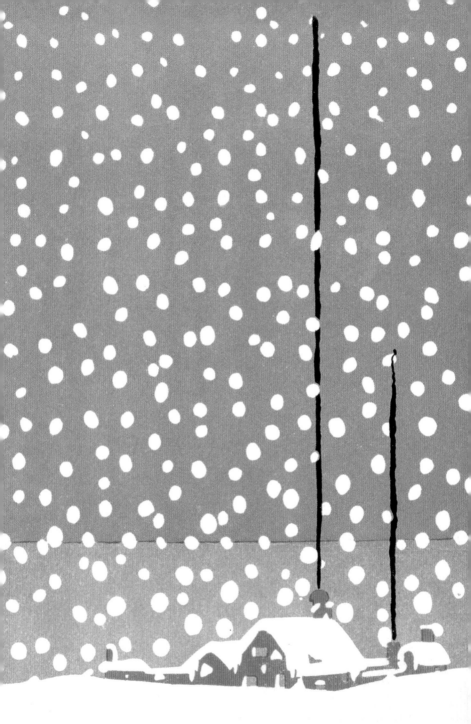

The lovely shapes and sounds intelligible
Of that eternal language, which thy God
Utters, who from eternity doth teach
Himself in all, and all things in himself.
Great universal Teacher! he shall mould
Thy spirit, and by giving make it ask.

Therefore all seasons shall be sweet to thee,
Whether the summer clothe the general earth
With greenness, or the redbreast sit and sing
Betwixt the tufts of snow on the bare branch
Of mossy apple-tree, while the nigh thatch
Smokes in the sun-thaw; whether the eave-drops fall
Heard only in the trances of the blast,
Or if the secret ministry of frost
Shall hang them up in silent icicles,
Quietly shining to the quiet Moon.

Samuel Taylor Coleridge
(1772–1834)

# The Barefoot Boy

Blessings on thee, little man,
Barefoot boy, with cheek of tan!
With thy turned-up pantaloons,
And thy merry whistled tunes;
With thy red lip, redder still
Kissed by strawberries on the hill;
With the sunshine on thy face,
Through thy torn brim's jaunty grace;
From my heart I give thee joy,—
I was once a barefoot boy!
Prince thou art,—the grown-up man
Only is republican.
Let the million-dollared ride!
Barefoot, trudging at his side,
Thou hast more than he can buy
In the reach of ear and eye,—
Outward sunshine, inward joy:
Blessings on thee, barefoot boy!

Oh for boyhood's painless play,
Sleep that wakes in laughing day,
Health that mocks the doctor's rules,
Knowledge never learned of schools,
Of the wild bee's morning chase,
Of the wild-flower's time and place,
Flight of fowl and habitude
Of the tenants of the wood;
How the tortoise bears his shell,
How the woodchuck digs his cell,
And the ground-mole sinks his well;

How the robin feeds her young,
How the oriole's nest is hung;
Where the whitest lilies blow,
Where the freshest berries grow,
Where the ground-nut trails its vine,
Where the wood-grape's clusters shine;
Of the black wasp's cunning way,
Mason of his walls of clay,
And the architectural plans
Of gray hornet artisans!
For, eschewing books and tasks,
Nature answers all he asks;
Hand in hand with her he walks,
Face to face with her he talks,
Part and parcel of her joy,—
Blessings on the barefoot boy!

Oh for boyhood's time of June,
Crowding years in one brief moon,
When all things I heard or saw,
Me, their master, waited for.
I was rich in flowers and trees,
Humming-birds and honey-bees;
For my sport the squirrel played,
Plied the snouted mole his spade;
For my taste the blackberry cone
Purpled over hedge and stone;
Laughed the brook for my delight
Through the day and through the night,
Whispering at the garden wall,
Talked with me from fall to fall;
Mine the sand-rimmed pickerel pond,

Mine the walnut slopes beyond,
Mine, on bending orchard trees,
Apples of Hesperides!
Still as my horizon grew,
Larger grew my riches too;
All the world I saw or knew
Seemed a complex Chinese toy,
Fashioned for a barefoot boy!

Oh for festal dainties spread,
Like my bowl of milk and bread;
Pewter spoon and bowl of wood,
On the door-stone, gray and rude!
O'er me, like a regal tent,
Cloudy-ribbed, the sunset bent,
Purple-curtained, fringed with gold,
Looped in many a wind-swung fold;
While for music came the play
Of the pied frogs' orchestra;
And, to light the noisy choir,
Lit the fly his lamp of fire.
I was monarch: pomp and joy
Waited on the barefoot boy!

Cheerily, then, my little man,
Live and laugh, as boyhood can!
Though the flinty slopes be hard,
Stubble-speared the new-mown sward,
Every morn shall lead thee through
Fresh baptisms of the dew;
Every evening from thy feet
Shall the cool wind kiss the heat:

All too soon these feet must hide
In the prison cells of pride,
Lose the freedom of the sod,
Like a colt's for work be shod,
Made to tread the mills of toil,
Up and down in ceaseless moil:
Happy if their track be found
Never on forbidden ground;
Happy if they sink not in
Quick and treacherous sands of sin.
Ah! that thou couldst know thy joy,
Ere it passes, barefoot boy!

John Greenleaf Whittier
(1807–1892)

# Catrin

I can remember you, child,
As I stood in a hot, white
Room at the window watching
The people and cars taking
Turn at the traffic lights.
I can remember you, our first
Fierce confrontation, the tight
Red rope of love which we both
Fought over. It was a square
Environmental blank, disinfected
Of paintings or toys. I wrote
All over the walls with my
Words, coloured the clean squares
With the wild, tender circles
Of our struggle to become
Separate. We want, we shouted,
To be two, to be ourselves.

## II

Neither won nor lost the struggle
In the glass tank clouded with feelings
Which changed us both. Still I am fighting
You off, as you stand there
With your straight, strong, long
Brown hair and your rosy,
Defiant glare, bringing up
From the heart's pool that old rope,
Tightening about my life,
Trailing love and conflict,
As you ask may you skate
In the dark, for one more hour.

Gillian Clarke

(1937– )

# The Land of Counterpane

When I was sick and lay a-bed,
I had two pillows at my head,
And all my toys beside me lay
To keep me happy all the day.

And sometimes for an hour or so
I watched my leaden soldiers go,
With different uniforms and drills,
Among the bed-clothes, through the hills;

And sometimes sent my ships in fleets
All up and down among the sheets;
Or brought my trees and houses out,
And planted cities all about.

I was the giant great and still
That sits upon the pillow-hill,
And sees before him, dale and plain,
The pleasant land of counterpane.

Robert Louis Stevenson
(1850–1894)

# I Remember, I Remember

I remember, I remember
The house where I was born,
The little window where the sun
Came peeping in at morn;
He never came a wink too soon,
Nor brought too long a day;
But now, I often wish the night
Had borne my breath away!

I remember, I remember
The roses, red and white,
The violets, and the lily-cups,—
Those flowers made of light!
The lilacs where the robin built,
And where my brother set
The laburnum on his birthday,—
The tree is living yet!

I remember, I remember
Where I was used to swing,
And thought the air must rush as fresh
To swallows on the wing;
My spirit flew in feathers then,
That is so heavy now,
And summer pools could hardly cool
The fever on my brow!

I remember, I remember
The fir trees dark and high;
I used to think their slender tops
Were close against the sky:
It was a childish ignorance,
But now 'tis little joy
To know I'm farther off from heav'n
Than when I was a boy.

**Thomas Hood**
(1799–1845)

# Infant Sorrow

My mother groan'd, my father wept;
Into the dangerous world I leapt,
Helpless, naked, piping loud,
Like a fiend hid in a cloud.

Struggling in my father's hands
Striving against my swaddling bands,
Bound & weary, I thought best
To sulk upon my mother's breast.

When I saw that rage was vain,
And to sulk would nothing gain,
Turning many a trick & wile,
I began to soothe & smile.

And I sooth'd day after day
Till upon the ground I stray;
And I smil'd night after night,
Seeking only for delight.

And I saw before me shine
Clusters of the wand'ring vine,
And many a lovely flower & tree
Stretch'd their blossoms out to me.

**William Blake**
(1757–1827)

# Children, Children

Children, children,
the dull and the clever
like a tide coming in
for ever and ever.

Children, children
ugly ones and pretty ones
Children, children,
country ones and city ones.

Each of them someone's son or daughter
leaping and shining like restless water
mouths and noses, eyes and ears
ready for laughter, ready for tears:

minds and bodies always moving:
where do they come from? They come from loving.

All those heads
and all those faces
they come from loving
in secret places:

from heat of love
all were begotten:
from love still burning
or love forgotten.

John Wain
(1925–1994)

# A Cradle Song

Sleep, Sleep, beauty bright
Dreaming o'er the joys of night.
Sleep, Sleep: in thy sleep
Little sorrows sit & weep.

Sweet Babe, in thy face
Soft desires I can trace
Secret joys & secret smiles
Little pretty infant wiles.

As thy softest limbs I feel
Smiles as of the morning steal
O'er thy cheek & o'er thy breast
Where thy little heart does rest.

O, the cunning wiles that creep
In thy little heart asleep.
When thy little heart does wake,
Then the dreadful lightnings break.

From thy cheek & from thy eye
O'er the youthful harvests nigh
Infant wiles & infant smiles
Heaven & Earth of peace beguiles.

William Blake

(1757–1827)

# Children's Song

We live in our world,
A world that is too small
For you to stoop and enter
Even on hands and knees,
The adult subterfuge.
And though you probe and pry
With analytic eye,
And eavesdrop all our talk
With an amused look,
You cannot find the centre
Where we dance, where we play,
Where life is still asleep
Under the closed flower,
Under the smooth shell
Of eggs in the cupped nest
That mock the faded blue
Of your remoter heaven.

R.S. Thomas
(1913–2000)

# in Just—

in Just—
spring when the world is mud—
luscious the little
lame baloonman

whistles far and wee

and eddieandbill come
running from marbles and
piracies and it's
spring

when the world is puddle-wonderful

the queer
old baloonman whistles
far and wee
and bettyandisbel come dancing

from hop-scotch and jump-rope and

it's
spring
and
the

goat-footed

baloonMan whistles
far
and
wee

e.e. cummings
(1894–1962)

# The Child on the Cliffs

Mother, the root of this little yellow flower
Among the stones has the taste of quinine.
Things are strange to-day on the cliff. The sun shines so bright,
And the grasshopper works at his sewing-machine
So hard. Here's one on my hand, mother, look;
I lie so still. There's one on your book.

But I have something to tell more strange. So leave
Your book to the grasshopper, mother dear,—
Like a green knight in a dazzling market-place—
And listen now. Can you hear what I hear
Far out? Now and then the foam there curls
And stretches a white arm out like a girl's.

Fishes and gulls ring no bells. There cannot be
A chapel or church between here and Devon,
With fishes or gulls ringing its bell,—hark!—
Somewhere under the sea or up in heaven.
'It's the bell, my son, out in the bay
On the buoy. It does sound sweet to-day.'

Sweeter I never heard, mother, no, not in all Wales.
I should like to be lying under that foam,
Dead, but able to hear the sound of the bell,
And certain that you would often come
And rest, listening happily.
I should be happy if that could be.

Edward Thomas

(1878–1917)

# Seven Yere of Age

(in the Middle Ages)

Aha, Wanton is my name!
I can many a quaynte game.
Lo, my toppe I dryve in same,
Se, it torneth rounder!
I can with my scorge-stycke
My felowe upon the heed hytte,
And lyghtly from hym make a skyppe;
And blere on hym my tonge.
If brother or syster do me chyde
I wyll scratche and also byte.
I can crye, and also kyke,
And mock them all berewe.
If fader or mother wyll me smyte,
I wyll wrynge with my lyppe;
And lyghtly from hym make a skyppe;
And call my dame shrewe.
Aha, a newe game have I founde:
Se this gynne it renneth rounde;
And here another have I founde,
And yet mo can I fynde.
I can mowe on a man;
And make a lesynge well I can,
And mayntayne it ryte well than.
This connynge came me of kynde.

Ye, syrs, I can well gelde a snayle;
And catche a coew by the tayle;
This is a fayre connynge!
I can daunce, and also skyppe;
I can playe at the chery pytte;
And I can wystell you a fytte,
Syres, in a whylowe ryne.
Ye, syrs, and every day
Whan I toscole shall take the waye
Some good mannes gardyn I wyll assaye,
Perys and plommes to plucke.
I can spye a sparowes nest.
I wyll not go to scole but whan me lest,
For there begynneth a sory fest
Whan the mayster sholde lyfte my docke.
But syrs, what I was seven yere of age,
I was sent to the Worlde to take wage.
And this seven yere I have been his page
And kept his commaundment...

Anonymous

# At the Sea-side

When I was down beside the sea
A wooden spade they gave to me
To dig the sandy shore.
My holes were empty like a cup,
In every hole the sea came up,
Till it could come no more.

### Robert Louis Stevenson
#### (1850–1894)

# The Poet at ten years old

from: The Prelude

Fair seed-time had my soul, and I grew up
Fostered alike by beauty and by fear:
Much favoured in my birth-place, and no less
In that beloved Vale to which erelong
We were transplanted;—there were we let loose
For sports of wider range. Ere I had told
Ten birth-days, when among the mountain slopes
Frost, and the breath of frosty wind, had snapped
The last autumnal crocus, 'twas my joy
With store of springes o'er my shoulder hung
To range the open heights where woodcocks run
Along the smooth green turf. Through half the night,
Scudding away from snare to snare, I plied
That anxious visitation;—moon and stars
Were shining o'er my head. I was alone,
And seemed to be a trouble to the peace
That dwelt among them. Sometimes it befell
In these night wanderings, that a strong desire
O'erpowered my better reason, and the bird
Which was the captive of another's toil
Became my prey; and when the deed was done
I heard among the solitary hills
Low breathings coming after me, and sounds
Of undistinguishable motion, steps,
Almost as silent as the turf they trod.

William Wordsworth
(1770–1850)

# A child said,
# What is the grass?

A child said, What is the grass? fetching it to me with full
    hands;
How could I answer the child?... I do not know what it
    is any more than he.

I guess it must be the flag of my disposition, out of hopeful
    green stuff woven.

Or I guess it is the handkerchief of the Lord,
A scented gift and remembrancer designedly dropped,
Bearing the owner's name someway in the corners, that we
    may see and remark, and say Whose?

Or I guess the grass is itself a child... the produced babe
    of the vegetation.

Or I guess it is a uniform hieroglyphic,
And it means, Sprouting alike in broad zones and narrow
    zones,
Growing among black folks as among white,
Kanuck, Tuckahoe, Congressman, Cuff, I give them the
same, I receive them the same.

And now it seems to me the beautiful uncut hair of graves.

Tenderly will I use you curling grass,
It may be you transpire from the breasts of young men,
It may be if I had known them I would have loved them;
It may be you are from old people and from women, and
    from offspring taken soon out of their mother's laps,
And here you are the mother's laps.

This grass is very dark to be from the white heads of old
    mothers,
Darker than the colorless beards of old men,
Dark to come from under the faint red roofs of mouths.

O I perceive after all so many uttering tongues!
And I perceive they do not come from the roofs of mouths
    for nothing.

I wish I could translate the hints about the dead young men
    and women,
And the hints about old men and mothers, and the offspring
    taken soon out of their laps.

What do you think has become of the young and old men?
What do you think has become of the women and
  children?

They are alive and well somewhere;
The smallest sprouts show there is really no death,
And if ever there was it led forward life, and does not wait
  at the end to arrest it,
And ceased the moment life appeared.

All goes onward and outward... and nothing collapses,
And to die is different from what any one supposed, and
  luckier.

Walt Whitman
(1819–1892)

# At the Zoo

First I saw the white bear, then I saw the black;
Then I saw the camel with a hump upon his back;
Then I saw the grey wolf, with mutton in his maw;
Then I saw the wombat waddle in the straw;
Then I saw the elephant a-waving of his trunk;
Then I saw the monkeys—mercy, how unpleasantly they smelt!

William Makepeace Thackeray
(1811–1863)

# Fairground

Thumping old tunes give a voice to its whereabouts
long before one can see the dazzling archway
of colored lights, beyond which household proverbs
cease to be valid,

a ground sacred to the god of vertigo
and his cult of disarray: here jeopardy,
panic, shock, are dispensed in measured doses
by fool-proof engines.

As passive objects, packed tightly together
on Roller-Coaster or Ferris-Wheel, mortals
taste in their solid flesh the volitional
joys of a seraph.

Soon the Roundabout ends the clumsy conflict
of Right and Left: the riding mob melts into
one spinning sphere, the perfect shape performing
the perfect motion.

Mopped and mowed at, as their train worms through a tunnel,
by ancestral spooks, caressed by clammy cobwebs,
grinning initiates emerge into daylight
as tribal heroes.

Fun for Youth who knows his libertine spirit
is not a copy of Father's, but has yet to
learn that the tissues which lend it stamina,
like Mum's, are bourgeois.

Those with their wander-years behind them, who are rather
relieved that all routes of escape are spied on,
all hours of amusement counted, requiring
caution, agenda,

keep away:—to be found in coigns where, sitting
in silent synods, they play chess or cribbage,
games that call for patience, foresight, manoeuvre,
like war, like marriage.

W.H. Auden

(1907–1973)

# Ballroom Dancing Class

The little girls' frocks are frilly.
    The little boys' suits are blue.
On little gold chairs
They perch in pairs
    Awaiting their Friday cue.
The little boys stamp like ponies.
    The little girls coo like doves.
The little boys pummel their cronies
    With white, enormous gloves.
And overhead from a balcony
The twittering mothers crane to see.

Though sleek the curls
Of the little girls,
    Tossing their locks like foam,
Each little boy's tie
Has slipped awry
    And his hair forgets the comb.
He harks to the tuning fiddle
    With supercilious sneers.
His voice is cracked in the middle,
    Peculiar are his ears.
And little girls' mothers nod with poise
To distracted mothers of little boys.

Curtsying to the hostess,
    The little girls dip in line.
But hobbledehoy
Bobs each little boy,
    And a ramrod is his spine.

With little girls' charms prevailing,
  Why, as the music starts,
Are the little girls' mothers paling?
  And why do they clasp their hearts
When the hostess says with an arching glance,
'Let boys choose partners before we dance'?

Now little girls sway
Like buds in May
  And tremble upon the stalk.
But little boys wear
An arrogant air
  And they swagger when they walk.
The meagerest boy grows taller.
  The shyest one's done with doubt,
As he fingers a manful collar
  And singles his charmer out,
Or rakes the circle with narrowed eyes
To choose his suitable Friday prize.
While overhead in the balcony
The little boys' mothers smile to see
On razorless cheek and beardless chin
The Lord-of-Creation look begin.

Oh, little boys beckon, little girls bend!
And little boys' mothers condescend
(As they straighten their furs and pat their pearls)
To nod to the mothers of the little girls.

Phyllis McGinley
(1905–1978)

# Of the Boy and his Top

A little boy had bought a Top,
The best in all the toyman's shop;
He made a whip with good eel's skin,
He lash'd the top, and made it spin;
All the children within call,
And the servants, one and all,
Stood round to see it and admire.
At last the Top began to tire,
He cried out, 'Pray don't whip me, Master,
You whip too hard,—I can't spin faster,
I can spin quite as well without it.'
The little Boy replied, 'I doubt it;
I only whip you for your good,
You were a foolish lump of wood,
By dint of whipping you were raised
To see yourself admired and praised,
And if I left you, you'd remain
A foolish lump of wood again.'

(Explanation.)
Whipping sounds a little odd,
It don't mean whipping with a rod,
It means to teach a boy incessantly,
Whether by lessons or more pleasantly,
Every hour and every day,
By every means, in every way,
By reading, writing, rhyming, talking,
By riding to see sights, and walking:
If you leave off he drops at once,
A lumpish, wooden-headed dunce.

John Hookham Frere
(1769–1846)

# There Was a Child Went Forth

There was a child went forth every day,
And the first object he look'd upon, that object he became,
And that object became part of him for the day or a certain
part of the day,
Or for many years or stretching cycles of years.

The early lilacs became part of this child,
And grass and white and red morning-glories, and white
and red clover, and the song of the phoebe-bird,
And the Third-month lambs and the sow's pink-faint litter,
and the mare's foal and the cow's calf,
And the noisy brood of the barnyard or by the mire of the
pond-side,
And the fish suspending themselves so curiously below
there, and the beautiful curious liquid,
And the water-plants, with their graceful flat heads, all
became part of him.

Walt Whitman
(1819–1892)

# The Children's Hour

Between the dark and the daylight,
When the night is beginning to lower,
Comes a pause in the day's occupations
That is known as the Children's Hour.

I hear in the chamber above me
The patter of little feet,
The sound of a door that is opened,
And voices soft and sweet.

From my study I see in the lamplight,
Descending the broad hall stair,
Grave Alice, and laughing Allegra,
And Edith with golden hair.

A whisper, and then a silence:
Yet I know by their merry eyes
They are plotting and planning together
To take me by surprise.

A sudden rush from the stairway,
A sudden raid from the hall!
By three doors left unguarded
They enter my castle wall!

They climb up into my turret
O'er the arms and back of my chair;
If I try to escape, they surround me;
They seem to be everywhere.

They almost devour me with kisses,
Their arms about me entwine,
Till I think of the Bishop of Bingen
In his Mouse-Tower on the Rhine!

Do you think, O blue-eyed banditti,
Because you have scaled the wall,
Such an old moustache as I am
Is not a match for you all?

I have you fast in my fortress,
And will not let you depart,
But put you down into the dungeon
In the round-tower of my heart.

And there will I keep you forever,
Yes, forever and a day,
Till the walls shall crumble to ruin,
And moulder in dust away!

Henry Wadsworth Longfellow
(1807–1882)

# Dirty Jim

There was one little Jim
'Tis reported of him,
    And must be, to his lasting disgrace,
That he never was seen
With his hands at all clean
    Nor yet ever clean with his face.

His friends were much hurt
To see so much dirt,
    And often they made him quite clean;
But all as in vain,
He was dirty again,
    And not at all fit to be seen.

When to wash he was sent,
He reluctantly went,
    With water to splash himself o'er.
But he seldom was seen
To have wash'd himself clean,
    And often looked worse than before.

The idle and bad,
Like this little lad,
    May be dirty and black, to be sure;
But good boys are seen,
To be decent and clean,
    Altho' they are ever so poor.

Jane Taylor
(1783–1824)

# My Parents Kept Me from Children who were Rough

My parents kept me from children who were rough
Who threw words like stones and who wore torn clothes.
Their thighs showed through rags. They ran in the street
And climbed cliffs and stripped by the country streams.

I feared more than tigers their muscles like iron
Their jerking hands and their knees tight on my arms.
I feared the salt coarse pointing of those boys
Who copied my lisp behind me on the road.

They were lithe, they sprang out behind hedges
Like dogs to bark at my world. They threw mud
While I looked the other way, pretending to smile.
I longed to forgive them, but they never smiled.

Stephen Spender
(1909–1995)

# In My Two Small Fists

in that bright blue summer
I used to gather
daisies for my father
speedwell for my mother

with buttercups
and prickly heather
cowrie shells
and a seagull's feather

treasures in each fist
all squashed together
daisies for my father
speedwell for my mother

  (that's how I see it
  but I don't know
  if it really happened
  sixty years ago

  but my memories shine
  and their light seems true
  and so do the daisies
  and speedwell too)

Adrian Mitchell
(1932–2008)

# My Lost Youth

Often I think of the beautiful town
That is seated by the sea;
Often in thought go up and down
The pleasant streets of that dear old town,
And my youth comes back to me.
And a verse of a Lapland song
Is haunting my memory still
'A boy's will is the wind's will,
And the thoughts of youth are long, long thoughts.'

I can see the shadowy lines of its trees,
And catch, in sudden gleams,
The sheen of the far-surrounding seas,
And islands that were the Hesperides
Of all my boyish dreams.
And the burden of that old song,
It murmurs and whispers still:
'A boy's will is the wind's will,
And the thoughts of youth are long, long thoughts.'

I remember the black wharves and the slips,
And the sea-tides tossing free;
And the Spanish sailors with bearded lips,
And the beauty and mystery of the ships,
And the magic of the sea.
And the voice of that wayward song
Is singing and saying still:
'A boy's will is the wind's will,
And the thoughts of youth are long, long thoughts.'

I remember the bulwarks by the shore,
And the fort upon the hill;
The sunrise gun, with its hollow roar,
The drum-beat repeated o'er and o'er,
And the bugle wild and shrill.
And the music of that old song
Throbs in my memory still:
'A boy's will is the wind's will,
And the thoughts of youth are long, long thoughts.'

I remember the sea-fight far away,
How it thundered o'er the tide!
And the dead captains, as they lay
In their graves, o'erlooking the tranquil bay
Where they in battle died.
And the sound of that mournful song
Goes through me with a thrill:
'A boy's will is the wind's will,
And the thoughts of youth are long, long thoughts.'

I can see the breezy dome of groves,
The shadows of Deering's Woods;
And the friendships old and the early loves
Come back with a Sabbath sound, as of doves
In quiet neighborhoods.
And the verse of that sweet old song,
It flutters and murmurs still:
'A boy's will is the wind's will,
And the thoughts of youth are long, long thoughts.'

I remember the gleams and glooms that dart
Across the school-boy's brain;
The song and the silence in the heart,
That in part are prophecies, and in part
Are longings wild and vain.
And the voice of that fitful song
Sings on, and is never still:
'A boy's will is the wind's will,
And the thoughts of youth are long, long thoughts.'

There are things of which I may not speak;
There are dreams that cannot die;
There are thoughts that make the strong heart weak,
And bring a pallor into the cheek,
And a mist before the eye.
And the words of that fatal song
Come over me like a chill:
'A boy's will is the wind's will,
And the thoughts of youth are long, long thoughts.'

Strange to me now are the forms I meet
When I visit the dear old town;
But the native air is pure and sweet,
And the trees that o'ershadow each well-known street,
As they balance up and down,
Are singing the beautiful song,
Are sighing and whispering still:
'A boy's will is the wind's will,
And the thoughts of youth are long, long thoughts.'

And Deering's Woods are fresh and fair,
And with joy that is almost pain
My heart goes back to wander there,
And among the dreams of the days that were,
I find my lost youth again.
And the strange and beautiful song,
The groves are repeating it still:
'A boy's will is the wind's will,
And the thoughts of youth are long, long thoughts.'

### Henry Wadsworth Longfellow
(1807–1882)

# The Schoolboy

I love to rise in a summer morn
When the birds sing on every tree;
The distant huntsman winds his horn,
And the sky-lark sings with me.
O! what sweet company.

But to go to school in a summer morn,
O! it drives all joy away;
Under a cruel eye outworn,
The little ones spend the day
In sighing and dismay.

Ah! then at times I drooping sit,
And spend many an anxious hour,
Nor in my book can I take delight,
Nor sit in learning's bower,
Worn thro' with the dreary shower.

How can the bird that is born for joy
Sit in a cage and sing?
How can a child, when fears annoy,
But droop his tender wing,
And forget his youthful spring?

O! father & mother, if buds are nip'd
And blossoms blown away,
And if the tender plants are strip'd
Of their joy in the springing day,
By sorrow and care's dismay,

How shall the summer arise in joy,
Or the summer fruits appear?
Or how shall we gather what griefs destroy,
Or bless the mellowing year,
When the blasts of winter appear?

Willam Blake
(1757–1827)

# A Medieval Schoolboy's Complaint

Hay, hay, by this day,
What availeth it me though I say nay?

I wold fain be a clerk,
But yet it is a stronge werk;
The birchen twigges be so sharp
It maketh me have a faint hert.
What availeth it me though I say nay?

On Monday in the morning when I shall rise,
At six of the clok, it is the gise
To go to scole without avise—
I had lever go twenty mile twise.
What availeth it me though I say nay?

My master looketh as he were mad:
'Where has thou be, thou sory lad?'
'Milke dukkes my moder bad'—
It was no mervaile though I were sad.
What availeth it me though I say nay?

My master pepered my ars with well good spede;
It was worse than finkell sede;
He wold not leve till it did blede—
Mich sorow have he for his dede!
What availeth it me though I say nay?

I wold my master were a watt,
And my book a wild catt,
And a brace of grehoundes in his topp:
I wold be glad for to see that!
What availeth it me though I say nay?

I wold my master were an hare,
And all his bookes houndes were,
And I myself a joly huntère
To blow my horn I wold not spare,
For if he were dede I wold not care.
What availeth it me though I say nay?

Anonymous

# from: On a Distant Prospect of Eton College

Say, father Thames, for thou has seen
Full many a sprightly race
Disporting on thy margent green,
The paths of pleasure trace;
Who foremost now delight to cleave,
With pliant arm, thy glassy wave?
The captive linnet which enthral?
What idle progeny succeed
To chase the rolling circle's speed,
Or urge the flying ball?

While some on earnest business bent
Their murm'ring labours ply
'Gainst graver hours that bring constraint
To sweeten liberty:
Some bold adventurers disdain
The limits of their little reign,
And unknown regions dare descry:
Still as they run they look behind,
They hear a voice in every wind,
And snatch a fearful joy.

Gay hope is theirs by fancy fed,
Less pleasing when possest;
The tear forgot as soon as shed,
The sunshine of the breast:
Theirs buxom health, of rosy hue,
Wild wit, invention ever new,

And lively cheer, of vigour born;
The thoughtless day, the easy night,
The spirits pure, the slumbers light,
That fly th' approach of morn.

Alas! regardless of their doom
The little victims play;
No sense have they of ill to come,
Nor care beyond to-day:
Yet see, how all around 'em wait
The ministers of human fate,
And black Misfortune's baleful train!
Ah, show them where in ambush stand,
To seize their prey, the murth'rous band!
Ah, tell them, they are men!

Thomas Gray
(1716–1771)

# A Fight at School

from: A Boy's Poem

Upon a day of wind and heavy rain
A crowd was huddling in the porch at school:
As I came up I heard a voice cry out,
'Ho, ho! here comes the lad that talks with ghosts
Sitting upon the graves.' They laughed and jeered,
And gathered round me in a mocking ring,
And hurt me with their faces and their eyes.
With bitter words I smote them in my hate,
As with a weapon. A sudden blow, and wrath
Sprang upward like a flame. I struck, and blood,
Brighter than rubies, gleamed upon my hand;
And at the beauteous sight, from head to heel
A tiger's joy ran tingling through my veins,
And every finger hungered for a throat.
I burst the broken ring, and darted off
With my blood boiling, and my pulses mad.
I did not feel the rain upon my face;
With burning mouth I drank the cooling wind;—
And then, as if my limbs were touched by death,
A shudder shook me, all the rage that sprang
Like sudden fire in a deserted house
Making the windows fierce, had passed away;
And the cold rain beat heavy on me now;
The winds went through me.

Alexander Smith
(1829–1867)

# from: Upon the Disobedient Child

Children become, while little, our delights!
When they become bigger they begin to fright's.
Their sinful nature prompts them to rebel,
And to delight in paths that lead to hell.
Their parents' love and care they overlook,
As if relation had them quite forsook.
They take the counsel of the wanton's, rather
Than the most grave instruction of a father.
They reckon parents ought to do for them,
Though they the fifth commandment do contemn;
They snap and snarl if parents them control,
Though but in things most hurtful to the soul.
They reckon they are masters, and that we
Who parents are, should to them subjects be!
If parents fain would have a hand in choosing,
The children have a heart will in refusing.
They'll by wrong doings, under parents gather,
And say it is no sin to rob a father.
They'll jostle parents out of place and power,
They'll make themselves the head and them devour.
How many children, by becoming head,
Have brought their parents to a piece of bread!
Thus they who, at the first, were parents' joy,
Turn that to bitterness, themselves destroy.

John Bunyan
(1628–1688)

# At School

from: A Boy's Poem

When but a trembling wind-flower of a child,
They set me in a large and crowded school.
The pale preceptor clad in rusty black,
The reading classes, and the murmuring forms
Were torture; and the ringing playground, hell.
I shrank from crowds of loud and boisterous boys.
The pain and forfeit of each game was mine;
Contempt, and scorn, and taunts were rained on me;
I wept within my little bed at night,
And wished that I were happy in my grave.
From out this depth of sorrow, slowly grew
A kindred and strange sympathy with eve,
With the unhoused and outcast winds, and with
The rain which I had heard so often weep
Alone, within the middle of the night,
Like a poor, beaten, and despisèd child
That has been thrust forth from its father's door.

Alexander Smith
(1829–1867)

# from: There Was a Boy

There was a Boy; ye knew him well, ye cliffs
And islands of Winander!—many a time,
At evening, when the earliest stars began
To move along the edges of the hills,
Rising or setting, would he stand alone,
Beneath the trees, or by the glimmering lake;
And there, with fingers interwoven, both hands
Pressed closely palm to palm and to his mouth
Uplifted, he, as through an instrument,
Blew mimic hootings to the silent owls,
That they might answer him.—And they would shout
Across the watery vale, and shout again,
Responsive to his call,—with quivering peals,
And long halloos, and screams, and echoes loud
Redoubled and redoubled; concourse wild
Of jocund din! And, when there came a pause
Of silence such as baffled his best skill:
Then, sometimes, in that silence, while he hung
Listening, a gentle shock of mild surprise
Has carried far into his heart the voice
Of mountain-torrents; or the visible scene
Would enter unawares into his mind
With all its solemn imagery, its rocks,
Its woods, and that uncertain heaven received
Into the bosom of the steady lake.

William Wordsworth
(1770–1850)

# American Boy

from: The Lost World

I wash my hands, Pop gives his pay
Envelope to Mama; we sit down to our meal.
The phone rings: Mrs Mercer wonders if I'd care
To go to the library. That would be ideal,
I say when Mama lets me. I comb my hair
And find the four books I have out: *The Food
Of the Gods* was best. Liking that world where
The children eat, and grow giant and good,
I swear as I've often sworn: '*I'll* never forget
What it's like, when *I've* grown up.' A prelude
By Chopin, hammered note by note, like alphabet
Blocks, comes from next door. It's played with real feeling,
The feeling of being indoors practicing. 'And yet
It's not as if—' a gray electric, stealing
To the curb on silent wheels, has come; and I
See on the back seat (sight more appealing
Than any human sight!) my own friend Lucky,
Half wolf, half police-dog. And he can play the piano—
Play that he does, that is—and jump so high
For a ball that he turns a somersault. 'Hello,'
I say to the lady, and hug Lucky... In my
Talk with the world, in which it tells me what I know
And I tell it, 'I know—' how strange that I
Know nothing, and yet it tells me what I know!—

I appreciate the animals, who stand by
Purring. Or else they sit and pant. It's so—
So *agreeable.* If only people purred and panted!
So, now, Lucky and I sit in our row,
Mrs Mercer in hers. I take for granted
The tiller by which she steers, the yellow roses
In the bud vases, the whole enchanted
Drawing room of our progress. The glass encloses
As glass does, a womanish and childish
And doggish universe. We press our noses
To the glass and wish: the angel—and devilfish
Floating by on Vine, on Sunset, shut their eyes
And press their noses to their glass and wish.

Randall Jarrell
(1914–1965)

# Floreat Etona

from: School and Schoolfellows

Twelve years ago I made a mock
Of filthy trades and traffics:
I wondered what they meant by stock;
I wrote delightful sapphics;
I knew the streets of Rome and Troy,
I supped with Fates and Furies,—
Twelve years ago I was a boy,
A happy boy, at Drury's.

Twelve years ago!—how many a thought
Of faded pains and pleasures
Those whispered syllables have brought
From Memory's hoarded treasures!
The fields, the farms, the bats, the books,
The glories and disgraces,
The voices of dear friends, the looks
Of old familiar faces!

Kind Mater smiles again to me,
As bright as when we parted;
I seem again the frank, the free,
Stout-limbed, and simple-hearted!
Pursuing every idle dream,
And shunning every warning;
With no hard work but Bovney stream,
No chill except Long Morning:

Now stopping Hatry Vernon's ball
That rattled like a rocket;
Now hearing Wentworth's 'Fourteen all!'
And striking for the pocket;
Now feasting on a cheese and flitch,
Now drinking from the pewter;
Now leaping over Chalvey ditch,
Now laughing at my tutor.

Winthrop Mackworth Praed
(1802–1839)

# Index to Poets

# Acknowledgements

WH Auden, 'Fairground' originally published in *The New Yorker* in 1966.
Reproduced with the kind permission of Curtis Brown.
John Betjeman, 'Hunter Trials' from *Collected Poems* (John Murray, 1979).
Reproduced with the kind permission of John Murray Publishers.
Gillian Clarke, 'Catrin' from *Collected Poems* (Carcanet, 1997).
Reproduced with the kind permission of Carcanet Press Limited.
Frances Cornford, 'On Children' from *Collected Poems* (Cresset Press, 1954).
Reproduced with the kind permission of the estate of Frances Cornford.
EE Cummings, 'in Just' reproduced with the kind permission of WW Norton.
Randall Jarrell, 'American Boy' from *The Lost World* (Eyre & Spottiswode Publishers, 1965).
Reproduced with the kind permission of the estate of Randall Jarrell.
Phyllis McGinley 'Ballroom Dancing Class' from *Times Three* (Viking Press, 1968).
Reproduced with the kind permission of Penguin Group USA.
Adrian Mitchell 'In My Two Small Fists' from *All Shook Up – Poems 1996 to 2000*
(Bloodaxe Books, 2000). Reproduced with the kind permission of United Agents
on behalf of the estate of the late Adrian Mitchell.
Stephen Spender, 'My Parents Kept Me from Children who were Rough' from
*Collected Poems 1928–1985* (Faber & Faber, 1989). Reproduced with the kind
permission of Ed Victor Agency.
RS Thomas, 'Children's Song' from *Collected Later Poems 1988–2000* (Bloodaxe
Books, 2004). Reproduced with the kind permission of Bloodaxe Books.
Anthony Thwaite, 'Child Crying'. Reproduced with the kind permission of
Curtis Brown.
John Wain, 'Children, Children' from *Professing Poetry* (Macmillan, 1979).
Reproduced with the kind permission of Macmillan Publishers Ltd.

# Picture Credits

Page 86 © Mary Evans Picture Library; Page 83 © Illustrated London News Ltd/Mary Evans; Page 56 © Mary Evans Picture Library/Peter & Dawn Cope Collection.
Pages 5, 22, 29, 35, 39, 46–47, 50, 64, 72–73, 91 and front cover © TfL from the London Transport Museum collection.
Pages 78–79 © National Railway Museum/Science & Society Picture Library; Pages 15, 16, 43, 53, 60–61, 69 © NRM/ Pictorial Collection/ Science & Society Picture Library.

Anova Books is committed to respecting the intellectual property rights of others. We have therefore taken all reasonable efforts to ensure that the reproduction of all contents on these pages is done with the full consent of the copyright owners. If you are aware of unintentional omissions, please contact the company directly so that any necessary corrections may be made for future editions.